# YOU GOT THIS!

A RISK-TAKING GUIDE FOR WOMEN WHO ARE READY TO CHANGE THE WORLD

MELANIE HARTH, PH.D., LPCC

*THE HAPPINESS DOC*

HW Media

Santa Fe New Mexico

Copyright © 2020 by Melanie Harth, Ph.D., LPCC.

All rights reserved. No part of this publication may be reproduced, distributed or transmitted in any form or by any means, including photocopying, recording, or other electronic or mechanical methods, without the prior written permission of the publisher, except in the case of brief quotations embodied in critical reviews and certain other noncommercial uses permitted by copyright law. For permission requests, write to the publisher, addressed "Attention: Permissions Coordinator," at the address below.

Melanie Harth Ph.D., LPCC/HW Media

P. O. Box 22852

Santa Fe, New Mexico USA 87505

Ordering Information:

Quantity sales. Special discounts are available on quantity purchases by corporations, associations, and others. For details, contact the "Special Sales Department" at the address above.

You Got This! A Risk-Taking Guide for Women Who Are Ready to Change the World/ Melanie Harth, Ph.D., LPCC. —1st ed.

ISBN 978-1-953449-02-3.

TABLE OF CONTENTS

WELCOME TO THE REST OF YOUR LIFE ............................................. 5
IT'S YOUR TURN ................................................................ 7
GETTING CURIOUS AND CREATIVE ................................................. 9
THINKING YOUR THOUGHTS ...................................................... 11
FEELING YOUR FEELS .......................................................... 13
OPENING TO VULNERABILITY .................................................... 15
TAKING ACTION ............................................................... 17
ONE SMALL THING ............................................................. 19
CERTIFICATE OF PERMISSION ................................................... 22
RESOURCES: PLAYSHEETS, PROMPTS, FEELINGS CHARTS ............................. 24
GRATITUDE ................................................................... 40

*This book is for all of the risk-takers, adventurers, explorers, fierce dream warriors, dedicated manifesters of magic, and determined-to-succeed souls who are ready to stop living small and scared, and start changing the world.*

CHAPTER ONE

Welcome to the Rest of Your Life

Is there something you want for yourself that somehow feels dangerous? Maybe a dream or desire that you don't think you're allowed to have? Something too big to even think about? Or so small and quiet that it's easy to brush it away, one more time.

That's a risk, just waiting for you.

You've been inundated with beliefs and stories and ideas about how the world is supposed to work, who you're supposed to be, and what your place in the family of things is supposed to look like.

Even good parents, teachers, family systems, communities, the culture in which you grew up, your ancestors … everyone's been bombarding you with stories about how things work.

All of those mixed-up messages and stories form subconscious beliefs and plain-wrong ideas when they're in conflict with who we are and what we want. This can result in a lot of confusion and drama.

All that drama? It's fantastic at sabotaging and suffocating all those sweet dreams and desires and goals.

Internal drama and confusion can manifest as anxiety, sadness, anger, fear, loneliness, and/or feeling like a victim or a martyr or an imposter (you know, those fun self-sabotaging archetypes).

External drama can include things like living in a garage when you're 40 years old, as Jen Sincero (*You Are a Badass*) writes and talks about. Or having to file bankruptcy because you were too scared to pay attention, as I did.

A wee bit too much wine or carbs or weed, hookups that go nowhere good, terrifying bank account balances … the list of ways that external drama plays out is endless.

Here's the thing. **Taking a risk means you have to walk toward the dangerous dream.** It's an act of faith that you'll be OK. Faith in the idea that won't leave you alone. In your longings and desires. In your own sweet self and what she wants.

As Jen Sincero said to me, "you have to want your dreams more than you want your drama."

Look at it this way. What happens if you don't take risks or go for your dreams, or shrug off those deep desires and sacred longings?

Nothing happens. If you really give zero f*#cks about deepening into yourself and what you're here to do, that is precisely the life you'll have.

A big, fat zero.

But that's not who you are, or you wouldn't be reading this book. Sure, you're scared. It's *scary* to make your own way sometimes, especially when "the voices around you [keep] shouting their bad advice," as poet Mary Oliver wrote in *The Journey*.

Does that mean you stay all small and scared or get so big and tough that no one can hurt you?

Nope. Not if you're ready to change the world.

This book is full of practices to help you dig deeper into your dreams and take more mindful risks. *Anyone* can learn them. And you'll be able to get started in like, two secs.

'Cause here's the thing -- we need you. We need you to come outside and be messy and brave and terrified, right alongside the rest of us.

These are transformational times. We're being called to step into our power, put on our superhero capes and fab protective cuff bracelets and gold sequined evening gowns or old faded jeans covered in paint and a t-shirt with no bra. We're it.

There's no more important journey to begin right now than that of taking more risks. We're leading the way for our daughters and sons and all the ones who are to come.

It's time to change the world. I'll help. Let's go.

Hugs all around,
Melanie, The Happiness Doc

CHAPTER TWO

It's Your Turn

The first time Jen Sincero, international bestselling author of the *You Are a Badass* empire, was on my radio show, she asked me if 90% of my job as a coach is just teaching people how to allow themselves to *be* who they already are.

It's *everything*, I answered.

When we laughed, there was a little bit of sadness around the edges. We knew how much gets lost when folks — including both of us — have learned to be afraid of who they are.

Another thing Jen said was, "if you're willing to do what it takes, you can have anything you want."

So how do you get started?

By taking the risk of giving yourself permission to be who you are and have what you want.

If you're already thinking, *"This is stupid." "Oh come on … what's she talkin' about?" "This isn't for me; this is for people who don't have a clue,"* for now, just hear those messages.

Those messages, your automatic thoughts, are just doing their job. Good to acknowledge them. But don't, not even for a New York minute, let those knee-jerk thoughts and subconscious beliefs make your choices for you.

Instead, **hang out with the idea that yes, you can actually have what you really want.**

## It's Your Turn
*Creative Resources, Ideas, Writing Prompts*

1. First, go to the Resources section in the back of this book, and find your Certificate of Permission.

Next, check out the *Ideas for Intentions, Affirmations, and Cognitive Reframe Ideas* on p. 24. Circle two or three that feel supportive or create a few of your own. If you craft your own, the only "rules" are:

- write them in present tense (I *am*, rather than I will or I want), and
- use positive language (*I'm doing this*, rather than *I'll never do that* or *I don't want this*).

Finally, fill out, sign and decorate your Certificate of Permission, repeating your affirmations as you do it. Create a little song of them, whisper them as a prayer to the Great What-*ever*, say them to yourself, yell them out loud. You're already re-wiring your brain for success.

Be playful. Make it beautiful. Use colored pens or pencils and stickers and gold stars and pink and purple hearts. Stay light, have fun with it!

2. Take a little walk with just yourself and your eagerness and the inevitable fears that always show up when we're staking a claim for ourselves. Let the fears be present, hear them, say hello. Make a list in your journal of what you hear.

3. At the end of the day, take a few quiet minutes to write down thoughts and feelings that showed up as you gave yourself permission to have or do or even *think* about what you want. Pay special attention to all the reasons you couldn't possibly do this. Use the play sheet on p. 25 to write down all your thoughts, feelings, and why-I-can'ts.

Hold onto your lists, you'll be coming back to them soon.

### writing prompt
Using the play sheet on p. 26, do a 15-minute write responding to this quote:

*"Don't ask yourself what the world needs. Ask yourself what makes you come alive and then do that. Because what the world needs is people who have come alive."* Howard Thurman

**podcast** with Jen Sincero www.melanieharth.com/jen-sincero-of-badass-fame

**book** *You Are a Badass*, Jen Sincero

CHAPTER THREE

Getting Curious and Creative

Any new choice is a risk.

After all, you're going for a brand-new thing as you make a creative new choice. Because of that, *any* risk can be looked at as an art-full one, no matter the size of the risk.

Being brave about a new haircut or color, crafting a business plan, going vegan, making a geographical move, falling in love or starting a family — all art-full creative risks.

Julia Cameron (author of *The Artist's Way* and 40+ more books) told me that "art is an act of expansion and faith."

Each risk is rich with the opportunity of expanding what you know, what you want, and what you do or don't like. And remember, it's built on the foundation of faith: in your idea, your goal, the dream, the abundant support of the universe. In yourself.

The expansion comes as we allow ourselves to grow into the dream of what we want, even when it doesn't seem possible. It's akin to the toddler proudly prancing around in mom's high heels who unfolds into the awkward teenager wearing what's cool, no matter what, finally growing into the woman who has her own collection of shoes.

Some of which might be thigh-high spike-heeled screaming red leather boots. Or a beloved pair of scuffed tennies that's been all over the world.

The faith part of what Julia said begins with that toddler's confidence that she, too, will one day walk in whatever danged shoes she wants to.

**There's an innocent, pure, precious, unbelievably strong, and confident energy that's very much alive within you.** That's the one who's the confident dream carrier.

This is a tender time in the world of imagining your future reality. Get curiouser and curiouser. Right now, just stay open to what wants to be seen and heard.

## Getting Curious and Creative
*Creative Resources, Ideas, Writing Prompts*

1. It's party time! Gather a few trusted friends, in person or virtually, and have a Visioning party. Play the game of What If … . *What if I had all the money I wanted? Could go anywhere? Do anything? My perfect life looks like … . Smells like? Feels like? Tastes like? Who's with me in my vision?*

Use the list of questions (p. 27), and do a playful timed write. Set a 5-minute timer for each prompt. If you're with friends, no sharing 'till it's over. You want your vision to be purely yours.

If you want to do this alone, cool beans.

2. Use visuals. Images without words are powerful for expanding the landscape of your imagination. Let your creative brain/mind *feel* into what's right for you without having words confine your heart's longings. You *want* your attention to be captivated by things your mind wouldn't usually register.
   - Vision-board it.
   - Tape or glue little pictures into your journal.
   - Spend an hour outside, taking smartphone shots of whatever catches your fancy.

Keep the energy moving. Keep it loose and light and fun. Keep opening the window of your playful curiosity and innovative creativity.

### writing prompts
Give yourself 8 minutes apiece for each of these prompts (p. 28).
   - *If it weren't so risky, I would try [list 10 things].*
   - *If it weren't so arrogant, I would try [name 10 things].*
   - *If it weren't so expensive, I would try [write down 10 things].*

[These ideas are "10 Things" from *The Artist's Way*; Julia Cameron calls it a portrait of your fears.]

Next, use the creative ideas that showed up for you as you explored all these things, and write the perfect storyline of the most remarkable life you can imagine for yourself (p. 29). Don't be practical. Don't go small. Go big, my friend.

**podcast** with Julia Cameron www.livingfromhappiness.libsyn.com/podcst/living-from-happiness-december-14-2016

**book** *The Artist's Way: A Spiritual Path to Higher Creativity*, Julia Cameron

CHAPTER FOUR

## Thinking Your Thoughts

You know that continually flowing river of judgey, shaming, self-defeating, negative thoughts? Welcome to your Monkey Mind. Constantly on the job, always vigilant to help you stay small and safe, Monkey Mind is one of the biggest obstacles to manifesting dreams, achieving goals, and holding a couple of stars in your hands.

Thoughts are tricky things. We need them. Thinking allows us to dive into our curiosity and use our imagination and creativity to fuel our risk-taking adventures. But we're not very good at discerning between the addictive, overthinking, fear-based Monkey Mind and our Wise Mind, the part of our minds that allows us to grow and deepen and expand into who we are beyond all that fear.

Wise Mind is our ally in taking good risks. Monkey Mind will try desperately to suffocate at least some of your dreams and desires.

When I talked with the clinical social worker and shamanic teacher Jose Luis Stevens, Ph.D., (*Awaken Your Inner Shaman: A Guide to the Power Path of the Heart*), he said that **"where your attention goes, so goes your power."**

If you were told that you couldn't write a book, or make a living as an artist, or that it's dangerous to travel around the world, or corporate life is terrible, or will never earn any money if you leave your day job and start your own little business, or that you simply can.*not* fully and fabulously embrace your weird (and who decided what "weird" is, anyway?!)?

If anybody told you anything negative about who you are, or what you want, part of you believed it. And that's where your attention goes, along with your power.

But here's the thing — *you* get to decide. You have to ... it's your life. These are *your* risks.

Shift your thoughts, change your world. Shift your mindset, claim your power. Shift your point of view, manifest your dreams.

## Thinking Your Thoughts
*Creative Resources, Ideas, Writing Prompts*

When you're learning to take more conscious risks, it's essential to let the voices of fear and self-doubt be heard. Go back to that list of thoughts and feelings that showed up in Chapter 1.

Add any others that've been showing up and need to be given some space.

Now, circle the ones that are jumping up and down right now. Edit the list down to the top 3-5 loudest, strongest, most insistent and demanding and familiar, negative, cannot-do-no-matter-what thoughts, ideas, and beliefs.

Finally, using the *Cognitive Reframes* play sheet on p. 30, reframe the loudest negative thoughts by flipping each one. What's the opposite? What's actually for-real true? Think of it as a coin — tails is the negative can't-do, heads is the reframe, or the positive oh-yes-I-can side.

Some examples are:
*I can't do that; he/she/they won't understand.*
  flip it: It's OK, I understand what I need. I wish them well, and I'm going for it.
*No way, they'll judge/shame/hate on me.*
  flip it: It's my life, my dream, my I-gotta-do-it thing. *I'm* showing up for me.
*Uh-uh, too scary.*
  flip it: It's OK that part of me is a little scared, *and* I'm moving ahead.
*Who do you think you are, Miss Fancy Pants?!*
  flip it: I'm smart/worthy/good enough/deserve this.
*Getting too big for your britches, girl.*
  flip it: I LOVE these britches.
*I'm way too busy/important/tired/poor/old/young.*
  flip it: I'm ready. Now is the perfect time. I have all the resources I need. Who I am and what I have is enough.
*I'm not ready!*
  flip it: I'm safe. I *want* this. It's OK; I'm always safe and protected, no matter what.

**podcast** with Pasha Hogan www.melanieharth.com/joy-is-not-meant-to-be-a-crumb

**book** *Mindset: The New Psychology of Success*, by Carol Dweck, Ph.D.

CHAPTER FIVE

Feeling Your Feels

All those thoughts you're thinking all day long? The ones we just talked about in the last chapter? They're triggering emotions ... all day long.

And those emotions feed the thought monsters that live in Monkey Mind, which then feed the emotion machine. Which keeps you from achieving goals and manifesting dreams.

Managing the feelings that *always* show up when we dare to challenge the edges of our known world is another big piece of successful risk-taking.

When I interviewed Amy McConnell Franklin, Ph.D., educator, author, speaker, change-maker, and expert in emotional intelligence and leadership, that's all we talked about.

Amy talked about the three levels of emotional intelligence:
1. accurately recognizing emotions;
2. navigating your own emotions;
3. knowing how to use emotions to motivate yourself and others.

Every thought triggers a chemical response in your nervous system. When the brain feels threatened — which it probably will when you're taking a risk — the limbic system takes over in a nano-second. It's that fight-flight-freeze response thing.

But there's another choice. **Consciously move toward the inevitable fear and doubt that's just part of taking a risk.**

That becomes possible when you
- let yourself be who you already are,
- honor what you want,
- hear the negative self-talk and internalized self-sabotaging beliefs,
- feel your feelings and don't run away, and
- course-correct your mind as many times as it takes to keep you on track.

You Got This!

## Feeling Your Feels
*Creative Resources, Ideas, Writing Prompts*

1. Using the Feelings charts (p. 31 & 32), take a few minutes to read through the lists. Look at how many ways there are to feel! And check out how many feelings can show up when your needs aren't satisfied.

That includes when you don't satisfy your own needs. **When an idea, a project, or a passion keeps getting shoved aside, you can build up a lot of negative emotions.**

For now, make a checkmark next to feelings that seem familiar. You'll be using these lists more when you begin crafting your One Small Thing plan.

2. Navigating your emotions, riding the waves of feelings, is a learnable skill. One of the most powerful ways to do that is to get quiet when your feelings are crashing around. Rather than avoiding them, pay a little attention to them for a little while. You'll begin noticing that feelings come and go, like the waves on a beach.

When you're learning how to take good risks on behalf of what and who you love … heads-up. Fear, boredom, self-dismissal, self-doubt, lack of self-confidence — *all* of them will show up. That's OK. The point is that you do not have to be at the mercy of those emotions. In fact, you can't be if you're going for it. One precludes the other.

Take a look at your *Cognitive Reframes* list from the last chapter. Read each negative thought, and then get curious about what feelings show up in response. Make a little note of them. Then read the positive, cognitive reframe sentence. Now, what feelings are showing up? Again, make a note of them.

You're learning to pay attention to these essential internal messengers, your feelings. Every time you pay attention, hear what you're telling yourself, and become aware of how that can trigger a feeling, you're getting stronger at taking risks. Every time you can question, even challenge an emotion that's holding you back, you earn 20 gold stars from the universe. Honest.

**writing prompt** Set the timer for 15 minutes. Write about a time you were a superhero (p. 33). Go!

**podcast** with Amy McConnell Franklin, Ph.D. www.melanieharth.com/emotional-intelligence.

**book** *Mindsight: The New Science of Personal Transformation*, Dr. Dan Siegel

CHAPTER SIX

Opening to Vulnerability

"Life can be lived without much heart, but what kind of life is it?" Licensed clinical social worker and shamanic teacher Jose Luis Stevens, Ph.D., asked that question on the air with me one day.

It's such a great question, isn't it? Most of us know how to do what needs doin' to get through the drudgery of our daily lives. But is that really enough?

When you begin activating your heart and mind in service of who you are and what you're here to do, it's part of the process to feel unsure and a little bit (or a lot) vulnerable.

You're in new territory, thank goodness. You don't *want* to recognize the landscape.

**And when you remember that part of risk-taking is learning to trust yourself, your ideas and dreams and that the universe has your back, the door opens to your sweet vulnerability.**

If you're a super-sensitive person, and/or already dealing with anxiety or depression, and/or have experienced trauma, your nervous system may be hyper-sensitive to feeling threatened. Taking a risk may activate some old stuff.

Adding to the fun, when we're learning something new, we're usually not very good at it. And the stakes feel higher when we go for something that matters to us. Along with the inevitable fears and doubts that show up whenever we decide to take a risk, we'll also feel a bit more vulnerable.

All of that's OK.

Vulnerability isn't an emotion. It's more like the roots of the emotional tree, with branches of shame, guilt, sadness, and anxiety. The way to work with your vulnerability is to keep opening your heart, one leaf at a time. One small thing at a time. This is what strengthens your roots, which strengthens the tree, which lessens the out-of-balance fears. Much better.

# Opening to Vulnerability
*Creative Resources, Ideas, Writing Prompts*

Sometimes we need a hug, or a lap to sit on, or a cup of hot chocolate or tea lovingly prepared for us in our favorite mug with just the right amount of honey to sweeten everything.

But what if there's no one around? Well then, we do it for ourselves. Here are some self-soothing ideas for you to explore when you're feeling a bit extra squishy.

- Gift yourself with a super-cuddly stuffed animal that's there for you, no matter what. Hug as often as needed. A friend taught me to do this; it helped me during a very rough time.
- If you're alone, see if there isn't one person, just one, who can support the risk you're going for, the *you* you're becoming. Oftentimes, there's someone waiting in the wings to be asked — a relative, a neighbor, a colleague. Also, consider making the investment in yourself and work with a counselor or coach (like me). Yes, asking = vulnerability. That's OK.
- Explore the free guided meditations on self-compassion and loving-kindness from Tara Brach, Ph.D.: www.tarabrach.com. Also, check out Dr. Kristen Neff's extensive free exercises: www.self-compassion.org/category/exercises/#exercises. These are like hugs for your mind.

### writing prompts
1. Make a list of what pumps you up (p. 34): doing an online training program, working with a coach, hanging out (online or as a podcast interviewer) with people who are already where you want to be, listening to music playlists or pods about what you're going for, interviews with experts, books galore, films/docs … whatever will keep inspiring and motivating you during those inevitable times when the self-doubt and negative self-talk start getting too loud.

2. Write a love letter to you, from your wise-woman self (p. 35). What does your inner wise-woman want you to understand? Read it whenever you're feeling especially negative about your dreams, goals, and desires.

**podcast** with Dr. Jose Luis Stevens www.livingfromhappiness.libsyn.com/podcast/living-from-happiness-april-18-2015-jose-stevens

**books and podcast**: Brene Brown is still the best www.brenebrown.com/

CHAPTER SEVEN

Taking Action

Risk-taking means *doing* things in new ways. Remember, anything unknown = scary to the brain. Which means you get to work with your brain in new ways. You've already been exploring tons of ideas in the earlier exercises.

The last step in taking that risk? Taking action.

Believe me, if I could think and wish and dream myself to a beautifully renovated beach cottage on the ocean, with very cool neighbors and the perfect wrap-around patio and plants that never got buggy, I'd be there right this second.

However. **Manifesting what we're dreaming about means we've gotta take more action than simply wishing and wanting while doing the same old/same old.**

Bill O'Hanlon is the author of 40+ books, a coach, hypnotherapist, psychotherapist, therapist trainer, musician and songwriter. When we talked on the air, he shared his 3-part formula for shifting out of the old can't-do neural grooves in the brain.

What you want to do, while you're developing your risk-taking skillset, is get *out* of the brain groove of familiar old self-defeating habits and negative associations.

- Change the doing.
    - Feeling blocked with your writing? If you usually write on the computer, write only with a pen and paper. *Do* it differently.
- Change the viewing.
    - View the risk you want to take from the present, as it is right now. Stop your brain from living in the past, when something didn't work. The past is over. Re-train it away from rehearsing a fearful future. Bring it into the present.
- Change the context.
    - Been trying to lose 10' indoors on a stationary bike, and it isn't working? Fast walk outside with a playlist to keep you moving, thereby changing the context of how you're going for the goal.

## Taking Action
*Creative Resources, Ideas, Writing Prompts*

At this point, you've got a tremendous amount of information, all written down on the play sheets or in your journal. The almost-final step is to create your action plan.

Go back and read through all of your writing prompts, every idea and thought about dreams and longings and goals. Circle or highlight every one of them using your favorite colored pen or pencil or glitter pen.

Using the play sheet on p. 36, write down one idea that's singing to you right now. Give it all your love as you begin to breathe life into this sacred dream.

Using the second half of that page, confidently record the affirmations and intentions that you'll be using to keep your risk-taking actions healthy and strong and moving forward.

Now, on another page, write down the loudest fears about doing it, along with the positive cognitive reframes for each one (p. 37).

And if you're feeling a little adrenaline rush, a little fluttering in your belly or energetic heart, that's terrific. That's good, healthy, eager, scared-excited energy. Onward.

You're 98% of the way there!

The last step is to take your idea/dream/desire/wish and begin breaking it down into action steps. Here are some of the things you'll be thinking about as you do that.

1. What: Name the Idea/Dream/Bihag (Big Hairy Audacious Goal).
2. When: When will you know it's done; what's the completion date?
3. How: Work backward, filling in the action steps to get you from where you are right now, today, to that future completion date.
4. Add markers all along the way so you keep yourself on track: small-task completion dates, weekly meetings with accountability buddies, celebrations, and positive neural reinforcements *every time* you take a baby step forward.
5. Set yourself up for success. When will you take the very first action step? Put it on the calendar. Who will be your support? Send an email, text, or make the phone call.
6. Go, my friend, go. The play sheet in the next chapter breaks it down even more.

**podcast** with Bill O'Hanlon www.melanieharth.com/make-positive-changes/

**book** *Do One Thing Different*, Bill O'Hanlon

CHAPTER EIGHT

One Small Thing

Now it gets real. Now's the time to stay accountable. No matter the size of the risk, staying on track is supported by things like productivity markers and calendar dates and accountability buddies.

In the case of risk-taking, size is in the eye of the beholder. My teeny tiny risk might feel like summiting Mt. Everest to you. It depends a lot on your comfort zone. If you're new to taking conscious risks, just as you're new at the local gym, start small. After all, your personal trainer isn't going to tell you to bench press 100' your first week.

You're in training to strengthen your positive, can-do, mindset muscles. You want to pay attention in a new way to how fearful thoughts, emotional responses to those thoughts and the brain's built-in negativity bias have all been holding you back.

You're going to start using your new skills to work with what shows up *while* you're taking action. You'll gently stimulate your feelings of vulnerability.

You're increasing your self-confidence, self-esteem, positive mindset, and upping your success factor by, like, 1000%.

As you get psychologically stronger and healthier and gain experience with how your nervous system reacts when you're taking a risk, you'll then start taking bigger leaps of faith, trying scarier things.

And all along, you'll understand that not a single one of these risks is actually, for reals, literally life-threatening. (Well, you know, unless you're going to be jumping out of planes or something. Even then, you'll undergo the training necessary to keep yourself safe, right?)

Action is the step that teaches you, and continually reinforces the truth, which is that you're safe. You're safe in who you are, and what you want for yourself and your precious life.

## One Small Thing
*Creative Resources, Ideas, Writing Prompts*

Calling in that big beautiful brain of yours, and inviting your heart into the conversation, get quiet with all you've learned about yourself and fill in the *I Want, I Will, I Need* play sheet (p. 38).

You've chosen the risk you want to take, and whether or not it's a Very Big Idea or a sweet little thing, you now get to break it down into actionable baby steps. **All you need to do is move it along an inch at a time.**

Heads-up: the brain *loves* to complete tasks. Checklists are great. Gold stars are groovy.

Therefore, celebrating the completion of each step is crucial. Reinforcing the positive is a critical step in strengthening the neural connections in your brain.

See? There are super-important reasons to happy dance, hug yourself, pat yourself on the back (literally hug yourself and say "pat, pat, pat"), treat yourself.

Once you've done it, taken one tiny step forward, rest for a sec in your accomplishments.

Water the new flowers you've just planted in your garden of manifesting dreams and achieving goals.

And then? Do it again. Take another step. **Keep moving forward … that's where your future is.**

The good news is that we're always becoming. Always strengthening and refining and flowing with the river of life.

It's why you're here, my friend.

## *Certificate of Permission*

By all the authority granted to me, because it's my life and these are my dreams and aspirations and goals, I hereby gift myself with permission to


- be who I am,

- have what and who I want,

- do what it takes to be successful in going after whatever the hell I choose.


_____  _____
*signature*                                                                                                  *date*

## Ideas for Intentions and Affirmations

My idea is potent and powerful.
It's OK to have what I want.
I know what I need and I'm willing to go after it.
I LOVE my idea.
It's my turn.
I'm worth the risk of going after my dreams.
I'm worth having what I want.
It's exciting to try out new things.
I'm loving myself into my future.
Trying new things lights me up … bring it on!
The freedom to be myself is fantastic.
I'm here to get some sh*# done. Let's go!
Transformation and innovative adaptation are saving the world.
Personal transformation makes the world a better place.
I'm handling my fears in brand-new ways that are deeply satisfying.
Taking risks keeps me emotionally strong and mentally healthy.
I'm showing my kids, friends, colleagues, the world how to do it, and I love that.
It's so cool being an explorer.
New adventures totally float my boat.
Everything is possible.
Oh, yes I can. Sure I can!
I love making good changes.
I love changes that make my life better.
Taking smart risks brings me alive.
I got this!
I friggin' got this!

head's-up: Neuroscience says intentions, affirmations and cognitive reframes need to be present tense, and positive. That's what helps reinforce the healthy neural connections in your brain.

Make your own list. Then write them on stickies and post them everywhere in the house, your car, on your computer. Set a timer for 60 minutes. Every time it goes off, take a 1-minute strength-training break, and whisper, shout, sing, dance 5-6 affirmations.

# Thoughts, Feelings, Fears & Why I Can'ts

You Got This!

## What Makes Me Come Alive

# What if … ?

What if I had all the money I wanted?

What if I could go anywhere?

What if I could do anything?

My perfect life looks like …

Smells like?

Feels like?

Tastes like?

Who's with me in my vision?

## 10 Things

If it weren't so risky, I would try …

1.
2.
3.
4.
5.
6.
7.
8.
9.
10.

If it weren't so arrogant, I would try …

1.
2.
3.
4.
5.
6.
7.
8.
9.
10.

If it weren't so expensive, I would try …

1.
2.
3.
4.
5.
6.
7.
8.
9.
10.

# My Most Remarkable Life

# Cognitive Reframes

# Feelings when your needs are satisfied

**AFFECTIONATE**
compassionate
friendly loving open
hearted
sympathetic
tender
warm

**ENGAGED**
absorbed
alert
curious
engrossed
enchanted
entranced
fascinated
interested
intrigued
involved
spellbound
stimulated

**HOPEFUL**
expectant
encouraged
optimistic

**CONFIDENT**
empowered
open
proud
safe
secure

**EXCITED**
amazed
animated
ardent
aroused
astonished
dazzled
eager
energetic
enthusiastic
giddy
invigorated
lively
passionate surprised
vibrant

**GRATEFUL**
appreciative
moved
thankful
touched

**INSPIRED**
amazed
awed
wonder

**JOYFUL**
amused
delighted
glad
happy
jubilant
pleased
tickled

**EXHILARATED**
blissful
ecstatic
elated
enthralled
exuberant
radiant
rapturous
thrilled

**PEACEFUL**
calm
clear
headed
comfortable
centered
content
equanimous
fulfilled
mellow
quiet
relaxed
relieved
satisfied
serene
still
tranquil
trusting

**REFRESHED**
enlivened
rejuvenated
renewed
rested
restored
revived

You Got This!

## Feelings when your needs are not satisfied

**AFRAID**
apprehensive

dread
foreboding
frightened mistrustful
panicked
petrified
scared
suspicious
terrified
wary
worried

**ANNOYED**
aggravated
dismayed
disgruntled
displeased
exasperated
frustrated
impatient
irritated
irked

**ANGRY**
enraged
furious
incensed
indignant
irate
livid
outraged
resentful

**CONFUSED**
ambivalent
baffled
bewildered
dazed
hesitant
lost
mystified
perplexed
puzzled
torn

**DISCONNECTED**
alienated
aloof
apathetic
bored
cold
detached
distant
distracted
indifferent
numb
removed
uninterested
withdrawn

**DISQUIET**
agitated
alarmed
discombobulated
disconcerted
disturbed
perturbed
rattled

**EMBARRASSED**
ashamed
chagrined
flustered
guilty
mortified
self-conscious

**FATIGUE**
beat
burnt out
depleted
exhausted
lethargic
listless
sleepy
tired
weary
worn out

**PAIN**
agony
anguished
bereaved
devastated
grief
heartbroken
hurt
lonely
miserable
regretful
remorseful

**SAD**
depressed

**TENSE**
anxious
cranky
distressed distraught
edgy
fidgety
frazzled
irritable
jittery
nervous
overwhelmed
restless
stressed out

**VULNERABL E**
fragile
guarded
helpless
insecure
leery
reserved
sensitive
shaky

**YEARNING**
envious
jealous
longing
nostalgic
pining
wistful

© 2005 by Center for Nonviolent Communication
Website: www.cnvc.org | Email: cnvc@cnvc.org
Phone: +1.505.244.4041

I was a superhero that time when ....

## Things That Keep Me Pumped

# Letter From My Wise-Woman Self

# The Idea That's Singing to Me
## *and*
## Positive Intentions & Affirmations

# The Loudest Fears & Positive, Cognitive Reframes for My Idea

## I Want, I Will, I Need

I want ...
_____
_____
_____.

I will complete this on or before _____.

I hereby grant myself permission to breathe life into my idea, to let my fears into the room, but not fall down the rabbit hole of self-sabotage. I'm using my affirmations and intentions and cognitive reframes to keep my mind focused and strong. I agree _____.

My One Small Thing plan includes these to-do's:
_____
_____
_____
_____
_____
_____
_____
_____
_____
_____
_____
_____
_____.

Add the completion date next to each of the to-do's.

My allies and angels and supporters are:
_____
_____
_____
_____.

When I need some help, I will ask _____.

I commit to taking the first step/s on or before _____.

If I get stuck, I'll send Melanie an email and ask for help. I agree _____.
melanie@melanieharth.com

## Gratitude

I'm so grateful for so much and so many! Thank you to the guests on my public radio show who make risk-taking easy, including Julia Cameron, Amy McConnell Franklin, Bill O'Hanlon, Pasha Hogan, Jen Sincero, and Jose Luis Stevens.

Endless gratitude to the global way-showers who continue to inspire, motivate and show me how to stand tall in the face of overwhelming risks.

- Pakistani activist Malala Yousafzai, shot in the side of the head when she was 15 years old for daring to speak out in support of girls attending school.
- Greta Thunberg, the Swedish climate activist who started an international climate strike movement for students all by herself when she was 15 years old.
- The Parkland, Florida high school students who survived a horrendous mass shooting and offered the world a model of collective healing and social activism.
- The artists of the International Folk Art Market in Santa Fe, New Mexico, who continually astound me with their resilience and dedication to their communities and countries through crafting hand-made beauty year after year.
- The artists at The Living Museum in Queens, New York, who showed me how to step into myself as an artist.
- The social justice movements that continue to teach by example, such as #MeToo, #BlackLivesMatter, #MomsDemandAction, and #SunriseMovement.

To the teachers who continue to help me better understand the world, including Brene Brown, Tara Brach, the psychological trauma specialists, positive psychology researchers, and happiness experts, thank you.

Shout-out to the biz coaches and dream inspirers who've kept me moving forward with my own risk-taking, including Dan Blank at www.wegrowmedia.com, Hiro Boga, Jason Buccholz at KN Literary Arts, Alexandra Franzen, and Bill O'Hanlon.

A special dance of happy gratitude goes to Alex Franzen and Lindsey Smith, at www.tinybookcourse.com, for getting me across this book's finish line.

Finally, my beloved son, I bow in your general direction.

www.ingramcontent.com/pod-product-compliance
Lightning Source LLC
Chambersburg PA
CBHW061106070526
44579CB00011B/151